Girl Talk

Girl Talk

CONNECTING THE HEART OF A WOMAN
TO THE HEART OF GOD

BY
PEGGY ASHMAN

ISBN: 978-0-9968250-0-9

Published and printed in the United States of America by the Write Place. Cover design by Tracy Watkins and interior design by Michelle Stam, the Write Place. For more information, please contact:

the Write Place
709 Main Street, Suite 2
Pella, Iowa 50219
www.thewriteplace.biz

Copies of this book may be ordered from the Write Place online at www.thewriteplace.biz/bookstore.

Dedication and Introduction

For all the amazing women I have had the pleasure of meeting, and those I have only read about.

Thank you for sharing your lives with me.

I invite you into the "corners of my heart"...and then we'll talk...
girl talk!

Nothing Wasted

Beautiful words from another dear sister…

"If God is real and true, and deeply involved in the details of my life, then ALL of my life was and is for something. Nothing is wasted."

Nothing to fear, sisters! Good things will come…because "He has a good plan for our life…a plan to prosper us and not to harm us…to give us hope and a future…"

Comfort Levels

Today, a sweet young gal asked: "Are you the most comfortable looking back where you have been? Standing right where you are? Or eager to run forward into what you don't yet know?" (Pretty awesome questions, from a gal at her young age!)

I thought I would throw the questions out to you all...good questions, aren't they! (Honestly, I am still pondering...)

Where IS my comfort?

Does it come from the "way things have always been"?

or

Am I only comfortable where I currently stand—not wanting to look back and too afraid to even imagine what is ahead? = "frozen"?

or

Am I definitely "over" the past, itching to get out of my "now"? Just try to hold me back from what I think I see way down the road ahead!

...a little grace for you ***and*** me on this one, sisters...knowing where our "comfort levels" are will help us when "new seasons" come...when we are faced with new opportunities or challenges...and in seasons of personal growth...

(Better get that second cup of coffee and read it over again...what do you see?)

The Ordinary

How often do we find ourselves tiring from the routine…struggling with the ordinary…looking for the fantastic?

I wonder if we could consider the Biblical donkey for just a moment… talk about an ordinary, boring, unattractive, unexciting animal…

BUT!

It was the lowly donkey that carried the King of Kings into a city that would soon mob and kill our Redeemer, changing forever the hope of the world!

Just your normal, average animal, ordinary by every standard…yet isn't it just like God to take that ordinary creation, from that ordinary environment, and make it extraordinary by the service it gives to others?

…A humble being doing what it was made to do…

…Let's think on this one, ladies…

His Power

Colossians 2:10
"Everything of God gets expressed in him, so you can see and hear him clearly. You don't need a telescope, a microscope, or a horoscope to realize the fullness of Christ, and the emptiness of the universe without him. When you come to him, that fullness comes together for you, too. His power extends over everything."

This verse speaks directly to the world we are living in.

"...the emptiness of the universe without him..."

No special lenses needed to see the emptiness, the brokenness that surrounds us today...

Praying for each of us to be drawn to Him ...

"...His power extends over everything!"

Position Yourself

I ran across a new phrase not long ago:

"Stand where fruit is falling"

I must admit, I had to stop and look at it for quite some time…what does this mean?

"Stand where fruit is falling"

Here is the definition given: "position yourself where the good stuff is. Find the goodness and get there…just get there! The goodness can only come when you are standing in the right place…"

There are clearly different points of interest in this phrase, but I am drawn to "position yourself"…what does this look like?

Allow me…what if you are in a "season of drought"? What if you are standing on "rocky ground"? Does it all go back to "I choose" or "I will"? Is the secret of abundance found in gratitude?

Daily gratitude?

A heart that truly rejoices in His loving kindness?

"Stand where fruit is falling"

Position yourself, dear sisters…

Oddball

How often have we felt that we need to get cleaned up, get on the right page, get our life in order before we can approach Jesus?

This is a lie, ladies!

Jesus actually went seeking the messy before they cleaned up anything at all. On purpose, Jesus went to the "less than desirable places" and talked with those who were thought less of. Jesus hung out with sinners, outcasts, the unworthy, and the scandalous.

Being the ***oddball*** that I am, I am so thankful that Jesus is no inspector of persons.

He loves us all anyway!

You may not fit into any of the categories listed above, but regardless, today, celebrate His love for you!

Wearing Our Faith

I think we would all agree that just because we are faithful in church attendance or our small group studies, or just because we wear religious jewelry, does not guarantee that we are "***faith full***."

Maybe a better way to wear our faith is with a healthy fear of God, a strong belief in a power much greater than our own, and by relying on that power in times of weakness and times of strength.

Wear your faith well, sweet sisters...

Trigger to Pray

Ladies, today, especially for each of you:

Philippians 1:6
"Every time you cross my mind, I break out in exclamations of thanks to God. Each exclamation is a trigger to prayer. I find myself praying for you with a glad heart. I am so pleased that you have continued on in this with us, believing and proclaiming God's Message, from the day you heard it right up to the present. There has never been the slightest doubt in my mind that the God who started this great work in you would keep at it and bring it to a flourishing finish on the very day Christ Jesus appears."

Blessings and hugs!

Thank You!

Psalm 138:1–3

"'Thank you!' Everything in me says 'Thank you'! Angels listen as I sing my thanks. I kneel in worship facing your holy temple and say it again: 'Thank you!' Thank you for your love, thank you for your faithfulness; most holy is your name, most holy is your word. The moment I called out, you stepped in; you made my life large with strength."

Yep, sisters, it's just one of those days…I can't say it enough: "Thank you!"

Pure Grace

Romans 12:3
"I'm speaking to you out of deep gratitude for all that God has given me, and especially as I have responsibilities in relation to you. Living then, as every one of you does, in pure grace. It's important that you not misinterpret yourselves as people who are bringing this goodness to God. No, God brings it all to you. The only accurate way to understand ourselves is by what God is and by what He does for us, not by what we are and what we do for Him."

Pure grace, ladies…it's nothing we are or what we do for Him…it's all about who He is and what He does for us.

Pure Grace

Pretending

Pretending to be okay does not make us okay.

Ladies, the truth is we are all broken in some way. Sometimes we recognize this brokenness, other times we just are not able to determine what causes that "rumble in our souls."

We have to admit, we can spend a lot of energy trying to hide it from everyone else. We have tried hiding it in:

Stuff – buying and then buying more
Food – because that is the one thing we think we can control
Relationships – good and bad ones
Ministry – busying ourselves – "being there for others"

The truth is, pretending—or hiding—did not work in the Garden of Eden and does not work any better for us today. The beauty is that God does not come at Adam and Eve with "Why?" He asks, "Where are you?" Isn't that because He already knows? He sees us as we are…He just wants us near Him.

Today, He is asking, "Where are you, dear one?" We need to hear God's love above the "noise of our guilt and shame" for who we think we are.

No more hiding…no more pretending…God sees you…and He loves you as you are.

What vs. Why

Have you found yourself in a situation where all you feel is "Why God? Why?"

God does not mind us asking Him "why"…He appreciates our honest, open-hearted conversation.

However, if the "why" draws us away from Him, it is probably not the right question at that time.

Maybe "what" is a better question. Like what should I be seeing or learning from this situation?

Isaiah 55:8
"I don't think the way you think.
The way you work isn't the way I work."
God's Decree.

There is just no way we can see the "big/full" picture as God sees it.

Our "whys" and our "whats" will be replaced by the truth of His Word.

And until we see "more clearly," let His truth get inside of you as deep as it can so it can achieve His purpose.

It's Enough

It is sad to see the walls go up around and between all of us:

Walls of "color"
Walls of nationalities
...so many, many walls...
And yes, even walls within the body of believers.

To be sure, these walls ***do*** make someone extremely happy and that is the devil himself. He knows that if he can divide, he can conquer.

And certainly the answer is not to fight the evil (the evil one) with more evil.

The only power that is able to hold us together is Jesus Christ.

This, dear sisters, is our only hope of unity:

Stand on the gospel of Jesus Christ.

It ***is*** enough!

Start to Finish

Matthew 5:16

"Now that I've put you there on a hilltop, on a light stand—shine! Keep open house; be generous with your lives. By opening up to others, you'll prompt people to open up with God, this generous Father in heaven."

How are you doing at seeing people the way God does?

Here is a little test to see where your heart is: the next person that sits next to you—what is your heart for them? Does the "outside package" matter too much to you?

The Biblical truth behind all of this is three points:
God's job is to judge.
The Holy Spirit's job is to convict.
Our job? ***To love.***

Start with love...finish with love.

Diversity

"Variety and diversity open our mind and heart to what we stand for."

What does that statement mean to you?

Reading that statement for the very first time, I felt that I would be offended, ***but...*** I actually feel something good about it. If we live in a world where decisions do not have to be made, when everything is the same for all, how do we know what we stand for...or do we even care? It is all too easy...there are no questions...

Knowing that there are so many choices to be made...so many different "gods" ready to be followed...I have found myself paying closer attention to what my faith in Jesus Christ really is...and what effect it has on this world...

Variety...diversity...hmmmmmm...

Jesus Christ

Everything

Matthew 22:37–40

"Jesus said, 'Love the Lord your God with all your passion and prayer and intelligence.' This is the most important, the first on any list. But there is a second to set alongside it: 'Love others as well as you love yourself.' These two commands are pegs; everything in God's Law and the Prophets hangs from them."

Everything…**EVERYTHING** hangs from those two things!

If "everything" is just too much to grasp, try it from this angle:
How can we hate when our eyes are full of His love?
How can our hands wound if they are full of His giving Spirit?

Love with your eyes.
Love with your hands.

Who's Driving?

Matthew 16:24–26
"Then Jesus went to work on his disciples. 'Anyone who intends to come with me has to let me lead. You're not in the driver's seat; I am. Don't run from suffering; embrace it. Follow me and I'll show you how. Self-help is no help at all. Self-sacrifice is the way, my way, to finding yourself, your true self. What kind of deal is it to get everything you want but lose yourself? What could you ever trade your soul for?'"

Sometimes it is just that plain, ladies…who's driving?

No Offense

Leviticus 19:18
"Don't seek revenge or carry a grudge against any of your people. Love your neighbor as yourself. I am God."

I was directed to an article that said "95% of the time when people say or do hurtful things, it really was not their intention to be hurtful." Most of the time they are acting under their own selfishness. So don't take offense. When we "hold or hide" offense in our heart, we are not able to minister to others.

Be free, ladies! Don't hold or hide that offense! Let it go!

Truth

Looking for truth?

Jesus said:

"I love you" – John 3
"I understand your rejection" – Isaiah 53
"I also was tempted" – Hebrews 4
"I want more for you" – Ephesians 3
"I will be here for you" – Romans 2

Through it all…through it all, my eyes are on you, Lord!

One More Thing

2 Thessalonians 3:1–2
"One more thing, friends; Pray for us. Pray that the Master's Word will simply take off and race through the country to a groundswell of response, just as it did among you. And pray that we'll be rescued from these scoundrels who are trying to do us in."

The day I read this verse was a "dark day" in the country I live in. Its words are so very real…**"these scoundrels who are trying to do us in"…**

Our response is so needed, sisters! **"Pray…pray that the Master's Word will simply take off and race through the country to a groundswell of response…and that we'll be rescued…"**

"One more thing," sisters: **"pray"!**

Faith Walk

"...walking on water is just the beginning."

I love this statement...stop and think about it...what goes through your mind?

Doubts?
Anxiousness?
Thrill?
Adrenaline?
Hope?
Expectation?

What has/does/will your "faith walk" look like?

Faith Out Loud

I read an article today that said (sadly enough) that "the number one reason that children walk away from the faith is that they never see it make a real difference in the lives of their parents."

How can this be?
Am I—as the parent—living my faith ***out loud***?
Have I told my children what I have and what I am praying for?
Have I shared with them how I can trace God's hand over my life?
Do we celebrate how God has blessed us…out loud?

Ladies, let's live our faith in such a way that God is too real to be denied!
Let them ***"see"*** our faith ***"out loud"***!

The Next Big Idea

Micah 6:8
"But he's already made it plain how to live, what to do,
what GOD is looking for in men and women.
It's quite simple: Do what is fair and just to your neighbor,
be compassionate and loyal in your love,
And don't take yourself too seriously—
take God seriously."

Sisters, let's not get so caught up in seeking the ***"next big thing"*** that we can do for God and miss the little things He has asked us to do.

"Act justly,
seek mercy,
walk humbly with your God."

Who's Calling?

Have you found yourself wondering…

Am I called to…?
Should I try…?
I feel I am being led to…

I have heard these questions often, when life changes or big decisions need to be made: **"How do I know this is from God?"**

I'm not saying this is always the case, but some things to consider:
Is serving someone involved?
Should I be an encouragement to someone else?
Am I being humbled?
Do I feel I am being led to give something away?

(If any of these things listed come into play, there is a good chance it is not the evil one calling you into it—he doesn't like any of those things.)

If you feel yourself wondering, it may be the perfect time for the "reason to" and the "reason not to" list. This list may give you the clear answer to "who is calling me?"

Family Circle

Revelation 5:9–10
"And they sang a new song:
'You are worthy to take the scroll, and to open the seals.
Because You were slaughtered, and You redeemed people
for God by Your blood from every tribe and language and people and nation. You made them a kingdom and priests to our God, and they will reign on the earth.' "

This morning I was blessed with a beautiful picture for my mind and my heart. I was watching a short video from a team that had been on a mission trip to another country. Each picture was only on the screen for a second or two, but one caught the eye of this "white woman from the center of this affluent USA." It was a scene of a "worship setting" in this foreign country. My eyes immediately were drawn to some writing on the wall in the background. The words were written in the native tongue, so I had no idea what they said, ***but*** behind the words was **"Ps. 37:4."** That is immediately familiar—MY LIFE VERSE!

As special as Psalm 37:4 is to me, God wrote it for ALL people—***"every tribe, every nation, every tongue!"***

I don't know if we will even recognize "skin tones" in Heaven, but this I know: surrounding the throne will be…***"every tribe, every nation, every tongue."***

God Is Able

If you could ask God for one thing, what would it be?
Physical healing?
Fix your finances?
Help you lead a loved one to Christ?
New job opportunity?
Mend a broken relationship?

How many of us believe, really believe in the deepest part of our heart that God really can do anything about it?
Have we asked God? Without giving up?

If we find ourselves doubting, even in the smallest way, ***remember***:
God created the world with His words.
He dropped food from Heaven, parted seas, and stilled storms.
He healed the sick, gave sight to the blind, and raised the dead.
He arose from death to life…

This is ***OUR GOD***!

Sisters, He ***IS*** able!

Memories

Today, as I worked away, feeling like I was totally committed to what had my attention, there was a lot of "noise," and yet from somewhere in the "air" came:

"Make some memories."

Immediately, I stopped, looked up to see where it came from…nothing there…yet, I heard it again…this time, from deep inside of me…

"Make some memories."

I think this is our word for today, ladies! In the midst of all the rush in each day,

STOP!

Take time,
be relational,
reach out,
celebrate.

"Make some memories!"

Full Lives

Ephesians 3:14–19

"My response is to get down on my knees before the Father, this magnificent Father that parcels out all heaven and earth. I ask him to strengthen you by His Spirit—not a brute strength but a glorious inner strength—that Christ will live in you as you open the door and invite him in. And I ask him that with both feet planted firmly on love, you'll be able to take in with all followers of Jesus the extravagant dimensions of Christ's love. Reach out and experience the breadth! Test its length! Plumb the depths! Rise to the heights! Live full lives, full in the fullness of God."

Ladies, what a beautiful Word! As it says;
"Reach out and experience the breadth!"
"Test its length!"
"Plumb the depths!"
"Rise to the heights!"
"Live full lives!"

LIVE FULL LIVES!

Tall Enough

Romans 15:7
"So reach out and welcome one another to God's glory.
Jesus did it: now you do it!"

I love this verse!

"welcome one another to God's glory"

Isaiah writes that the root of Jesse was a tree growing tall. Tall enough for everyone everywhere to see and take hope. What a beautiful testimony of a life well lived! I pray for each of you gals that your faith lives and that it is evident to those you rub shoulders with today.

A wonderful testimony of our faith well lived is if it ***welcomes someone to God's glory***. I pray our faith rises **tall enough** and that this is what others see when they look at us…not our faults…not our weaknesses…

"welcome one another to God's glory"

Invite Him

Sometimes the God of the universe pauses in the midst of all His creation to touch the heart of one person.

Today, He paused for you.

Ladies, today, invite God into the midst of your world. Invite Him into the struggles, the pain, the chaos…and most definitely into your celebrations, your joy, your gratitude…

Today, He paused for you!

We can only imagine what the power of God can do when we invite Him into our lives…

Today, He paused for you!

Less Is More

Today, ladies, I want you to focus on one thing:

You are a treasured child of the Most High God!

…to be repeated as many times as you want…or as you need today!

Dark Nights

"Even though I don't feel His presence, I will seek to love Him as He has never been loved."

– Mother Teresa

This quote from Mother Teresa jumped off the pages of a book I was reading, and I think it has been engraved forever somewhere in my heart. Mother Teresa said this during a time when she craved the voice of God and just felt like He must be "busy" in other places…in other lives…

…yet…

Mother Teresa kept on…she kept on doing Kingdom-building work… one touch…one word…one act of kindness…being the hands and feet of Jesus…showing His love…in every way she knew to ***"love Him as He has never been loved."***

If you are out there today, asking where in the world is God, or why does He not answer…sometimes, we just need something to do. So get busy, sisters…not just to be busy, but to do something for the Kingdom…maybe smile and say a kind word to the ignored…open a door for someone else to walk through…notice those who are struggling…maybe physically…maybe emotionally…maybe financially…

Love, sisters! Love with your words, with your hands, with your feet… ***"love Him as He has never been loved."***

Open My Eyes

Well, ladies, I absolutely have to go here today! It is one of my favorite "God stories" in the whole Bible!

2 Kings 6:15–17
"Early in the morning a servant of the Holy Man got up and went out. Surprise! Horses and chariots surrounding the city! The young man exclaimed, 'Oh, master! What shall we do?'
He said, 'Don't worry about it—there are more on our side than on their side.'
Then Elisha prayed, 'O God, open his eyes and let him see.'
The eyes of the young man were opened and he saw. A wonder! The whole mountainside full of horses and chariots of fire surrounding Elisha!"

And, as you'd guess, the servant then found nothing to fear.

Often times, we feel unable to handle the particular thing we face. Yet in our hearts we know that we should be able to because we know Christ lives in us. His power and protection surround us.

This day, my prayer for each of you who stops to read this is that the LORD will ***open your eyes!*** That you will fix your eyes on HIM and that the truth of HIS presence will be seen with your own eyes!

Liar! Liar!

In John 8:44, Jesus calls Satan the "father of lies," and here are three of his biggest lies:

...there is no strength to conquer the temptation facing us...
...peace is not possible...
...the mercy and love of God IS conditional, and that neither of them is forever...

To fight these lies and the many others that the father of lies throws at us, it is so very important to ***"let the word of Christ richly dwell in us" (Colossians 3:16).*** This means that when those lies jump in front of our mind and our heart, we want the truth of God's Words to flow ***reflexively*** from us.

This brings us back to the basics...the reading and memorizing of God's Word! I would love to know that His words are so much a part of me that when the father of lies hurls an untruth at me, the truth of God's Word has already covered my mind, my heart, AND my mouth!

"Let the word of Christ richly dwell in us."

Fruitfulness vs. "Busyness"

This is a good one, ladies! By "good" I mean one that we all can relate to! It's so very easy for us to fill our lives with all kinds of activities—whether of church, of home, of school, or of friends. So many things we can and are doing. But let's be careful not to confuse our busyness with our fruitfulness.

Being fruitful means to be productive and excellent in what you do. It isn't draining, it doesn't wear you out, and you don't have to force things to happen. There is peace and contentment in a fruitful life. It blesses others, and it receives God's blessings in return.

Does this "fruitful" description sound like your life? I'm certainly considering if it describes mine! Maybe we need a little of Psalm 46:10:

"Be still, and know that I am God: I will be exalted among the nations, I will be exalted in the earth."

Blessed fruitfulness, sisters!

Behold, Our God!

Let the whole world glorify His name.

This morning I have been contemplating what this phrase means in my life. I think most often I associate how I see God in nature with this one, but today He has taken it a step further…

Someone dear to me "saw Jesus" at a very early age during a revival meeting…

Another person close to me "saw Jesus" in a dream, where he heard God speaking to him…

And yet another "saw Jesus" during a near-death experience…

For myself, I "saw Jesus" through the teaching of His Word and through diligent studies.

Still there are others that "see Jesus" through the acts of love shown to them in defining moments…

Ladies, this is what it means to me to "let the whole world glorify His name."

Please don't discount the many ways that God reveals Himself to us all!

Behold, our God! Seated on His throne! Come let us adore Him!
Behold our God! Nothing can compare! Come let us adore Him!

A Salvation Garden

James 1:19–21
"Post this at all the intersections, dear friends: Lead with your ears, follow up with your tongue, and let your anger straggle along in the rear. God's righteousness doesn't grow from human anger. So throw all spoiled virtue and cancerous evil in the garbage. In simple humility, let our gardener, God, landscape you with the Word, making a salvation garden of your life."

As I finished up a weekend of landscaping, weed pulling, and "detailing" our garden in an effort to make it beautiful, this verse jumped out at me.

…the weed pulling…
…pruning…
…re-planting….

Can't think of a better picture of what God is doing in my life!

Waiting Well

Isaiah 64:4
"Since before time began no one has ever imagined, no ear heard, no eye seen, a God like you who works for those who wait for him."

We all know God could instantly step into a situation and change it. And many times He does. *BUT*, there are those other times where it seems God purposefully has us wait. Maybe because waiting calls us to walk in faith and hope…

Sisters, never fear that God is not working while you are waiting. We would be amazed if we could only see how He is moving everything into place, in its time! And not just so that it affects us, but so that many around us are affected as well!

These can be trying times of waiting, but here's a tip to help endure the wait: ask God to make you more aware of Him…better yet, ask Him to make you more aware than you have ***ever*** been…and then, ***HANG ON, sister!*** With everything you are, hold as tightly to Him as you're able. That puts you right next to Him. No better place to be!

Judge Not

Romans 14:10

"…so where does that leave you when you criticize a brother? And where does that leave you when you condescend a sister? I'd say it leaves you looking pretty silly—or worse. Eventually, we're all going to end up kneeling side by side in the place of judgment, facing God. Your critical and condescending ways aren't going to improve your position there one bit."

As the kids today say, BOOM! and I would add OUCH!
But this scripture is clearly here for our good, right?!

When I stand face to face with God, He isn't going to ask me about you…nor will He ask you about me. If He asks me why I wasn't willing to work with Him on my issues, I don't want to have to say, "Well, I was just so busy trying to fix everyone else's."

Romans 14 says we will each give an account of our own life before God. I know we aren't supposed to think of ourselves before others, but in this case, let's deal with our own issues and let others do the same.

(I think we all deserve a latte after this one!)

Let It Flow

1 Corinthians 1:10
"I have a serious concern to bring up with you, my friends, using the authority of Jesus, our Master. I'll put it as urgently as I can: You must get along with each other. You must learn to be considerate of one another, cultivating a life in common."

Ladies, I think as each of us reads this, faces begin to form in our minds. We all have someone who challenges us…and I don't think we need to go any further on that. But here it is…**"serious concern"** and **"urgent"**—we **"must get along"**…we "must learn to be considerate."

These words are not meant for us to glance at and walk away from… many times it feels like "the love" only flows in one direction…**so let it flow!**

Let His love flow through us…it will purify our heart as it reaches someone else…

Let it flow! Let it flow!

Consider

Romans 4:19–21
"Abraham didn't focus on his own impotence and say, 'It's hopeless. This hundred-year-old body could never father a child.' Nor did he survey Sarah's decades of infertility and give up. He didn't tiptoe around God's promise asking cautiously skeptical questions. He plunged into the promise and came up strong, ready for God, sure that God would make good on what he had said. That's why it is said, 'Abraham was declared fit before God by trusting God to set him right.' But it's not just Abraham; it's also us! The same thing gets said about us when we embrace and believe the One who brought Jesus to life when the conditions were equally hopeless. The sacrificed Jesus made us fit for God, set us right with God."

Consider Abraham…he had many reasons to waver in his belief of God's promises. Yet Abraham did not consider the reasons why he couldn't be the father of many nations. He considered God's faithfulness and chose to give Him glory and praise.

What are you believing God for? Does it seem impossible? Is it taking a long time? Consider God's ability over your circumstance!

Consider your God!

Consider His Word!

Consider His faithfulness!

Double for Your Trouble

Zecharíah 9:12

"Return to the stronghold, you prisoners of hope. Even today I declare that I will restore double to you."

Holding on to resentment, hurt, and anger can be like being in a prison.

Ladies, let go of it.

This verse says to walk away from it.

Step out of the prison and become a prisoner of hope.

Lock in to the attitude that God is your vindicator…that you will not be defeated.

Stay strong and grab on to the hope that you will come out with double for your trouble!

Bravo, God!

Psalm 47:4
"Applause, everyone. Bravo, bravissimo!
Shout God-songs at the top of your lungs!
God Most High is stunning,
astride land and ocean.
He crushes hostile people,
puts nations at our feet.
He set us at the head of the line,
prize-winning Jacob, his favorite.
Loud cheers as God climbs the mountain,
a ram's horn blast at the summit.
Sing songs to God, sing out!
Sing to our King, sing praise!
He's Lord over earth,
so sing your best songs to God.
God is Lord of godless nations—
sovereign, he's King of the mountain.
Princes from all over are gathered,
people of Abraham's God.
The powers of earth are God's—
He soars over all."

Ladies, this is the perfect song for us today! So let's come together, sisters! God gathers us together for this harmony of Heaven. He has made joyfulness from all the chaos that surrounds us!

How ***AWESOME*** is the Lord Most High!
Let's all say this out loud at least once today!
Chaos is defeated! God is the one true King of all the earth!
BRAVO! BRAVO!

Always Praise

Romans 11:33–36
"Have you ever come on anything quite like this extravagant
generosity of God, this deep, deep wisdom? It's way over
our heads. We'll never figure it out.
Is there anyone around who can explain God?
Anyone smart enough to tell him what to do?
Anyone who has done him such a huge favor
that God has to ask his advice?
Everything comes from him;
Everything happens through him;
Everything ends up in him.
Always glory! Always praise!
Yes. Yes. Yes."

Dear sisters, whether you are experiencing the darkness of the soul or singing songs of victory, take a minute to FEEL where you are…God's grace has found you and covers you…***"everything happens through Him."*** Breathe in His grace…let out your praise!

"Always glory! Always praise! Yes. Yes. Yes."

Challenge Yourself

Here is a powerful way to begin your day!

Challenge yourself with this thought:

What could I do today that would outlive anything the world would call an accomplishment?

Already that rules out most of what we thought would be important for us to do today! And I sense many of the items that were at the top of my "to-do list" for today suddenly slipping a bit farther down the list.

Maybe it helps to think of what will go with us into the next life…what comes to mind? First in my mind is "people"—so maybe that is involved in the importance of my day. Could be that "people" are the most obvious choice. What else?

You know, ladies, I'm just going to leave it right here…get yourself a good morning coffee, or in my case, the amazing latte…and let's all sit with this one a bit…

What could I do today that would outlive anything the world would call an accomplishment?

Do You Want It?

John 5:1–6

"Soon another Feast came around and Jesus was back in Jerusalem. Near the Sheep Gate in Jerusalem there was a pool, in Hebrew called Bethesda, with five alcoves. Hundreds of sick people—blind, crippled, paralyzed—were in these alcoves. One man had been an invalid there for thirty-eight years. When Jesus saw him stretched out by the pool and knew how long he had been there, he said, 'Do you want to get well?'"

Ladies, Jesus gets up close and personal with us today. He is asking us: ***Do you want to get well?***

Do you want to get rid of your fear?
Do you want to lose your negative attitude?
Do you want to forgive?
Do you want to enjoy eating and not let food control you?

Please don't miss the words just before "do you want to get well." Jesus ***"knew how long he had been there"!*** Jesus knows how long you have lived in fear…how long you have walked around with a chip on your shoulder…feeling offended and resentful…how long you have allowed food to control you…how long…**He knows!**

Jesus simply asks us, ***"do you want to get well?"*** Can it be this simple? Oh, sweet sisters, let's try to make it that simple…bring it before the Lord…really bring it this time. Invite Him completely into this area of your life…Jesus promises to meet our needs and to restore anything we have lost because of it.

Yes, Lord, I want to get well!

Healing for My Soul

Could it be, ladies, when we find ourselves a bit on the grumpy side, that maybe, just maybe the Holy Spirit is "dealing" with us? Could it just be something needs to get "squeezed out"?

I'm not saying this is always the case, but sometimes we just need to come clean before the Lord. Many faith leaders would call this "conviction." Although that doesn't sound like a "nice" word, it truly is one of the best words!

Conviction brings healing to my soul!

If there is something I am being convicted of, whether in thought, word, or actions, and I lay it before the Lord, it brings me back into agreement with God. Soon after, the grumpiness is lifted, my peace returns, and my behavior is much improved.

Sometimes we are well aware of the source of our grumpy nature, but for those times when you just can't seem to pinpoint the root of it, just ask the Holy Spirit to show you and to cleanse you of the seen and the unseen.

John 16:8
"Christ came to convict and convince us of our sin, without judgement!"

Sisters, today, let conviction bring healing to your soul…

Peace

Hold your peace!
It is important to recognize what situations get your blood boiling.

Some of us become easily upset when we are multitasking, while others do their best work handling many situations at one time.

Some of us let our children make and learn from their own choices, while others feel the need to step in and rescue them.

Some of us work better into the night when it is quiet, and others wake up with an energy to take on the world.

You may get upset or impatient with traffic, where I may take that time to just rest and reflect a bit.

If we stop for a second, I think each of us knows what brings us to the edge…what challenges our peace. Each of us has different triggers, and Satan knows what they are and how to use them to steal our peace.

I would encourage you to take notice of when you are feeling your peace fade…maybe track it for a while and see if a pattern comes to light…

Knowing and recognizing these moments—which may seem more like seasons at times—take the power from Satan and put it back in our hands.

When you feel a moment rising, recognize it…talk yourself through it…memorize a Bible verse or two to throw at the devil's attempt to steal your joy…and lighten up…smile at yourself… ***"the joy of the Lord is your strength"***…and ***hold your peace!***

It's a Praise Day

Psalm 103:1–2
"O my soul, bless God.
From head to toe, I'll bless his holy name!
O my soul, bless God,
don't forget a single blessing!"

I know that every day should be a "praise day," but, ladies, I am a work in progress, and it just doesn't play out that way for me. So, occasionally, I just declare the day a praise day! It isn't a national day, of course, and no one else needs to even take notice. It just brings so much resolution to my life. By that, I mean it brings peace in areas where I find anxiety in my life.

Psalm 103 is my favorite praise verse:

"O my soul, bless God. From head to toe, I'll bless his holy name!"

From head to toe, sisters! Start from your head and work all the way down to your toes! That is a full day of praise right there! For everything it takes for this physical body, not to mention what happens in my mind, what is happening in my heart, along with my busy hands, my feet, etc.…you've got the picture! And then, moving on to everything that comes my way.

By the end of this day, I feel like I have had the ultimate workout, and honestly, girls, you know how good that really feels! Even the most strenuous workouts leave you feeling peaceful, somehow. The same with this day of praise!

Give it a try, ladies! **A praise day**—for everything about you and your life! It will do your heart, soul, mind, and strength good!

Calm After the Storm

This is for the girls who have walked through a difficult time in their life. There are so many possibilities, but some storms that either I or someone close to me have recently walked through are:

- Child moving out
- Shocking health diagnosis
- Loss of a job
- Sudden death of a loved one

The emotional energy that it takes to pass through one of these storms and then the sudden stillness after can be overwhelming.

His grace is sufficient in our weakness.

Relax in the stillness.
Breathe deeply and hang on to His hand.
Take one step at a time.

To see your life after the storm has passed can be a strange feeling. The life you know now can be one of wondering: "will this...," "will they...," "will that..."?

Trust Him, sister! He is the One who carried you through the storm and the One who still clings to your hand. Rest in knowing He is strong when you are weak.

Take one step...you are already doing better than you thought you could...take another step...

Keep Walking

Psalm 23:4

"Even when the way goes through Death Valley, I'm not afraid when you walk at my side. Your trusty shepherd's crook makes me feel secure."

Sometimes, we just have to play in pain. We have to keep going even when we don't feel like it…keep pressing forward even when it's tough.

God sees the effort!

It's honorable, for sure, to do the right thing and make good decisions when everything is going our way. **BUT!** When times are tough, when you are hurting, when you should be on the sidelines, nursing your wounds but instead you are in the game:

You are still getting to work on time.
You are still being good to someone.
You are still expecting God to turn it around.
This, my friend, gets God's attention in a new way.

Quite possibly, God has a greater reward for those who are faithful through very difficult times.
If this is you today, know that God's hand is upon you!
Keep praising.
Keep believing.
Keep moving forward knowing that God is with you.

…keep walking…

Soul Friends

Each year as we celebrate the anniversary of our birth, we are blessed with texts, posts, phone calls, and visits from many people who have crossed our path. It is so special to reflect a bit on each person and how they have influenced us.

I believe God brings us "soul friends" to help us on our life's journey. Some come through predictable places: a small group, a friendship, a neighborhood, a club, or a mentorship.

But occasionally we find them in places we may not have expected. These soul friends may not even be aware that they have a deep impact on our growth or that they are being used as guides to help us on our journey of faith.

Whether they have been friends for many years or perhaps hidden guides, all are able to see us through eyes of grace that help us to take the next step on our journey of faith.

Take a moment to praise God for your soul friends! Whether they know it or not, they have been used to help guide you on your journey of faith.

Let Love Lead

Muscle can split a shield. It can even destroy a life. But only the unseen power of love can open the hearts of men.

– Og Mandino

Greet today with love!

What does this look like besides "being nice" and having a "sweet spirit"? Not to diminish the importance of either one of these attributes.

But what about the other areas of our life that we face? Here are some things to think on:

I wake up to see the sun—love it for its warmth.
I wake up to see rain—love it for its nourishment and its cleansing.
I have a busy day—I love it for the opportunities.
I have a slower day—I love it for the rest.
I will love ambition because it inspires me.
I will love failure because it teaches me.

This list goes on and on…you can always apply love to it.

What greets you today?

Let love be your guide today!

Lost and Found

We all know what it's like to lose something: keys, purse or wallet, an earring, an address…this list could go on and on…and we all have experienced the great joy and relief in finding what was lost!

My pastor had an amazing message based on Luke 15:1–7. You know this story: the shepherd goes out to find the one lost sheep out of the hundred that he owns. There were so many great points my pastor made in placing each one of us in this story, but I want to point out just two of them:

First, this story shows the "ownership" of the shepherd. The sheep that was lost ***belongs*** to the shepherd already. He was not just out there picking random animals—goats, cows, foxes, etc. God's effort is to restore something of His that is lost. This comforts me in a couple of situations in my life…the sheep has lost its way, but it has not been lost from the owner.

Secondly, God gives each of us an opportunity to reach out, to love, to pray for, to encourage, to genuinely show love to a lost sheep—maybe a bit more love than we have for those "not lost"!

Here it is, ladies: if you are feeling lost, maybe even just a little: stop! Turn around and see Jesus running toward you to rescue you!

If you are feeling safe and at home, don't be content to munch the green grass around you, or, as Luke 19:10 says, become ***"busy with our own righteousness."*** Be ready, be available, and be willing to love the lost one as Jesus brings that dear one home!

Just Watch

2 Chronicles 20:12
"We don't know what to do, but we look to you."

Does that sound anything like **"I don't know what else I can do. I'll just have to pray about it."** We say this often…I hear it often…**"all we can do is pray."**

2 Chronicles 20—I love this story of Jehoshaphat. He is facing a huge battle and he is questioning God…feeling insecure in his own strength…he says, "It doesn't look good here…I'm at the end of my rope."

In 2 Chronicles 20:15, God answers, ***"Do not be afraid or discouraged because of this vast number, for the battle is not yours but God's."*** And then my favorite, verse 17: ***"You do not have to fight this battle. Position yourself, stand still, and see the salvation of the Lord."***

What a beautiful picture when facing our battles…our challenges…our struggles:

Look to the Father—He is our defender, our protector—**it's His battle!**

I don't even have to fight! I just need to find a good spot and **watch!**

Hear my heart, sisters—I know many of you are walking UP huge mountains, and I don't want to minimize the toughness of your journey…but ladies, I didn't make this up…God has inspired these words for our good:

"Do not be afraid or discouraged."
"The battle belongs to God."
"Position yourself."
"See the salvation of the Lord!"

Pray Continually

1 Thessalonians 5:16–18
"Be cheerful no matter what; pray all the time; thank God no matter what happens. This is the way God wants you who belong to Christ Jesus to live."

Enjoyed a wonderful conversation with a sweet gal about prayer. Sometimes these conversations can reveal what you really believe inside. Just letting your heart have a voice can be amazing.

Here is what we discussed:

When you pray, you are not talking to yourself. You are talking to God, and He hears you! And responds! Remember, it is not your prayer that has the power, but it is our God on the other end of the line who has the power to do what we can't.

Prayer is so very important on our journey.

Please note that God has planned for us to be on a journey, ladies, not a race.
Not very many things change overnight. (Although some things change in an instant!)
Don't push it.
Give God time to work...and remember to be thankful for the changes that you see.

Admit It!

Matthew 5:3

"God blesses those who realize their need for him."

No matter what you are struggling against, God's power is available to you…to equip you to go beyond what you thought was possible.

He can get you through a painful event.

He can help you deal with that difficult relationship.

He can make that dream you've been holding on to come true.

Whatever it is, God will make a way for you. It may not look like you thought it would, but the moment you ask God for help, you are no longer limited to your own strength. You now are tapped into God's resources!

God does His best work when you are at the end of yourself—***and finally admit it.***

Changing Seasons

Ecclesiastes 7:14
"On a good day, enjoy yourself;
On a bad day, examine your conscience.
God arranges for both kinds of days
So that we won't take anything for granted."

Someone close to me asked, "How do you pick something to write about? Do you have resources?" Quick answers: the Bible and life.

Today's verse is exactly that…I began reading my Bible and this verse jumped off the page…and it feels a bit like my life (insert smiley face).

I would almost dare to assume that you are like me, in that some days it seems like all is right with the world and then other days—well, let's just say there are days that challenge me…can you relate?

This verse speaks over my life…

There will be some days when I can't stop smiling…**AND!** There will be tougher days—and on those days I need to look inside my mind to what is really troubling me…and then that smiley day comes again…and, OHHHHHH! The joy!

I picture this like people who live 365 days a year in sun and warm temps…soon they forget what it is like to experience 20-below wind chill and snow…and then we hear the words, "I miss the changing seasons where I live." Can we apply this to our faith—our walk also?

When we live in an unchanging atmosphere, we start to take things for granted…God allows for both good and tough times in our life…but always, ***always*** for our good and for His purpose.

On your journey, enjoy the "seasons" that keep you smiling and have faith to survive the "seasons" you struggle through.

Lagniappe

Once in a while I come across a word that just stops me in my tracks… welcome "lagniappe"!

Isn't that just the best-sounding word?

I like saying it…

It makes me smile…

Some words just do that…

They make you smile!

Lagniappe…and here's the meaning: it's a French word meaning "an extra unexpected gift," like the thirteenth doughnut when buying a dozen…

An extra unexpected gift…this is what I pray over your life today…from our Father. An extra unexpected gift…a little something extra…extra joy…extra peace…extra strength…for more than you asked for…for more than you need…for more than you dreamed of…"lagniappe"…a little something extra.

TODAY…straight from Ephesians 3…"for more than you dare to ask, or hope, or dream"…lagniappe!

Help My Unbelief

Do you remember the exchange Jesus had with the father who sought healing for his son?

Mark 9:23–24
"Jesus said, 'If? There are no 'ifs' among believers.
Anything can happen.'
No sooner were the words out of his mouth than the father cried,
'Then I believe. Help me with my doubts!'"

This could be the life verse for all of us who struggle with doubt. We know we believe, and yet there are still doubts.

But doubters, TAKE HEART! Doubt is not rejecting truth; it is questioning truth. To doubt is to leave room for greater belief! Isn't that a relief? Doubt is sin only if it leads to rejecting God. Otherwise, doubt is to question the truth of something!

So let's word it this way…"I know that I can experience much greater belief, but my doubts hold me back sometimes. Lord, help me with my doubts!"

Today let's receive much greater belief and push out the doubt.

You Are Important!

Jeremiah 29:11
"For I know the plans I have for you," says the Lord. "Plans to prosper you, not to harm you. To give you hope and a future." – NIV

The day you asked me to, I sat down and wrote this…

YOU were created for a reason. God made you, formed you. He has a good plan for your life. YOU are important to God, and that makes you important. Even if you don't accomplish something that makes headlines, you are still important to God.

But sometimes understanding that you ARE important helps you to go on to do great things. If you tell yourself you are going to do great things and be an influence, you most likely will.

Just remember you are stronger than you think. Don't give up too easily. Don't settle when, deep down, you know you can do more, give more. Surround yourself with people who believe in you.

Step out today, knowing YOU are important!

Ignorance Is NOt Bliss!

Romans 1 says that all of us have been born with a heart for "His Divine Being," so that no one has a good excuse for not being able to "see" Him.

Even though we know He is real, we have not always treated Him like God. We have refused to worship Him and traded the glory of God for cheap earthly imitations.

So God's response in Romans 1:24 is, "If that's what you want, that's what you get." And guess what follows…refuse to know God, and not long after we don't even know how to be decent to each other…evil breaks loose, envy, bickering, cheating, etc.…such darkness and more…and then we say, where is God?…why does He allow this?…could it be that if, in fact, He has withdrawn Himself a little, it just might be to make me desire His presence more? Or in other words, if God seems distant, who do you think moved?

Today, "Draw near to the Father, and He will draw near to you."

No Middle Ground

I heard a phrase over the weekend that is just sticking with me…I know I am supposed to mention it, but I just don't know where to go with it. This is the phrase:

"If we are not moving toward God, we are moving away from Him."

Even now as I read it in print, I'm still wondering what to do with it. Is it true? Is there no spot in the middle to rest? Can I just catch my breath from my arrival before I have to jump in and go deeper? It appears to be calm here, right now—can I just enjoy this? After all, the road ahead could be rough…it could cost me…

"If we are not moving toward God, we are moving away from Him."

Could it be that I lose intensity for Him while I am just resting? Do I begin to look around? Get interested in other things?

You know, I just don't have an answer on this one…I think the best thing is for you to "chew on it"…just as I have been the last few days…

Do you see this being true in your faith walk?

Do you desire to move towards Him?

Beautiful Mess

Walking through life together—friends, loved ones—is a beautiful thing, but it also has moments that are messier than others.

There is no formula or math equation that can keep relationships simple and straightforward.

We have all been there at times—when things get complicated, even frustrating…and not long after that, everything feels out of control.

Here is a key phrase that was spoken over me just today, actually: **"Humble yourself, and give up your right to be right."**

Really? Because what I want to do is argue, because I KNOW I'm right…

"Humble yourself, give up your right to be right."

Do something exactly the opposite of what you naturally want to do, and then just watch everything work out…

Can you hear the voice of God in this?

After all, what would He do? We know that answer…extend the hand of grace…in fact, extend both hands…

When our beautiful relationships get messy, let's look for the best and hope for the best, with strength to step back…to have loving respect and the ability to read each other's heart.

…maybe today…just step back…

Expect His Goodness

Psalm 34:1

"I will praise the Lord at all times. I will constantly speak his praises."

When you wake up in the morning, do you expect God's goodness in your life?

It doesn't matter what happened yesterday, or last year; today is a new day!

You may be surrounded with complainers, negative people full of discouragement, but don't let that rub off on you! Instead, choose to ***praise the Lord at all times.***

Let praise be like the light of dawn that shines brighter and brighter until it is the full sun. Be determined to set the tone for each new day! Speak words of faith over your future. Praise Him and make room for God to do amazing things in every area of your life!

I will praise the Lord at all times. I will constantly speak his praises!

Celebrate! Dance to the Music!

WOW! Just hearing the words to that song again takes me back to the 70s. It just makes you want to jump up and down.

Celebrate! Let's just make this a celebration day, shall we?!

Philippians 2 says, "Be glad and rejoice!"

Celebrate! I recently read about the "discipline of celebration." Seriously, do we need discipline to celebrate? Uuh, maybe so. Maybe it seems frivolous to celebrate…maybe we are in the middle of something messy or dealing with some serious challenges, so that we may not feel like rejoicing…

So maybe the discipline to celebrate IS needed…

"Be glad and rejoice"
in the mess
in the pain
let's dance anyway!

Let's choose to point out the beautiful things...
the sunrise
the smell of fresh-baked goodies
the smile from a friend...

God is at work in His world, even when we can't see it. He has created us to see the best, believe the best, even desire the best. This is what makes us different from the rest of the world…

"Be glad and rejoice"*...dance anyway!*

Leadership

When you get a chance, read through 1 Timothy 3—any version really. I think the "read" will be the same. This chapter talks about leadership in the body…some of the descriptions are:

- not pushy, but gentle
- not thin-skinned, not deceitful
- reverent before the mystery of the faith (one of my favorite descriptions!)
- dependable, not sharp-tongued
- diligent in looking after their own affairs
- a credit to this Jesus-faith

These are challenges for all of us…we are all leaders in arenas of many different kinds.

I don't feel like I am qualified to be considered in this chapter, but I know God has placed me in different arenas where I have the opportunity to influence…thus these challenges are for me…and for all of you.

Praying that others see Him in me…Lord help me.

Today Is Your Day

Psalm 118:24

"This is the day the Lord has made; we will rejoice and be glad in it." – NIV

How often do we find ourselves saying…
"Someday this problem will turn around."
"Someday we'll get a break."
"Someday I'll feel better."

How often are we putting our faith into the future?

But what about today?! Isn't our faith present for today? Isn't God the Great I Am? That sounds like now…today!

God wants to show us His goodness today! Yep, TODAY is your day! Today I will get the phone call I've been expecting! Today, my health improves! Today, my wandering child comes home!

TODAY!

Let's live in expectancy that today is the day! What is God doing TODAY?

Show Mercy

Romans 12:21
"Do not be overcome by evil, but overcome evil with good." – NIV

It takes a lot of humility to treat someone with respect who is disrespecting you. It is rarely easy; in fact, it's almost NEVER easy! Yet, His Word says, ***"overcome evil with good."***

So here is the deal. When you walk in humility, God gives you HIS grace! He empowers you to walk in HIS goodness. Let's receive HIS grace and HIS goodness, and in HIS strength we will be all He has called us to be!

So today, let's show mercy! And sow mercy!

Let's walk humbly with God and overcome evil with good.

Shake It Off

Isaiah 43:18–19

"Remember not the former things, nor consider the things of old. Behold, I am doing a new thing; now it springs forth, do you not perceive it? I will make a way in the wilderness and rivers in the desert." – ESV

Read it again, sweet sisters! It is truly one of my favorites!

"Behold, I am doing a new thing."

Sometimes we get stuck in life because we've been hurt or betrayed. We sit too long in our disappointment. Don't let what somebody did or didn't do for you be an excuse to live "sour."

Move forward, and God will take care of it. Move forward, and you'll come into a new beginning. Nothing that has happened to you is a surprise to God. Nothing has caught Him off guard.

So the real question is: are you going to get stuck in the past? Will you become bitter? OR, are you going to shake it off and move forward knowing that your best days are still ahead?

Shake it off, sisters!

No One Left Behind

Philemon. Yes, I said Philemon! Have you spent time in this "one-book wonder"? Paul writes from prison in this book, and you have to love his heart:

Receive each other in forgiveness and love.

Help each other feel useful in the body.

Encourage each other—even if we have walked a certain way for a time, or have had a dark season…to once again be useful in His Kingdom work.

It is what encouragers are called to do…make sure no one is left behind!

…holding hands and walking it out…

Style Show

Colossians 3:1
"So if you're serious about living this new resurrection life with Christ, act like it."

Oh, that I could be the person described in this chapter.

That I would not shuffle along, eyes to the ground, absorbed with the things right in front of me. But that I would look up and be alert to what is going on around Christ—that is where the action is. To see things from His perspective.

Verses 12–14 say, *"Dress in the wardrobe God picked out for you: compassion, kindness, humility, quiet strength, discipline. Be even-tempered, content with second place, quick to forgive an offense...And regardless of what else you put on, wear love."*

There it is…what to wear? Wear the wardrobe God has laid out for us… wear love!

My prayer is that people will see Christ through touching my life today… and the same for each of you!

The Journey Never Ends

I saw this phrase on an ad the other day, and it has just stuck with me… the truth behind these four words is incredible:

Our journey never ends!

So true! We certainly have a beginning, but once begun, we never end…am I the only one who just wants to sit with this thought for a bit? ***Our journey never ends!*** Praise God, right?! So many things do have an end:

Relationships
Years
Activities
The day, as well as the night
Even our hair has ends

I know that once I have excited this flame of thought in you, there are many, many things you are thinking of with ends—I would be interested to hear some of your more imaginative ones.

BUT! ***Our journey NEVER ends***…we begin this life, and on and on and on it goes…eternity…there is never an end…isn't that just amazing?! What a sweetness flows over my soul…when I pass from my earthly form, my spirit "simply" crosses over into eternity where there will be NO END!

This is clearly not earth-shattering to any of us, yet just let it cover your heart today! Put down any anxiousness that is coming at you…breathe…in and out…in Him…***your journey never ends***…

New Lenses

Today has special meaning for me…it is an anniversary of sorts…not one that anyone would welcome into their life, really, and yet it is a day that deserves to be remembered and almost cherished in a peculiar sort of way.

Here's the thing…have you ever felt that quite possibly you may have "smudged the lenses" of a loved one's life perspective with your own fears? If you can relate, please be aware that it will take time for them to see beyond the ground-in scratches of your own brokenness and get new lenses of their own.

For those of you who have in the past or are currently walking this path, I know you understand the symbolism…and hear my heart in this:

PRAYER MATTERS

PEOPLE MATTER

CHANGE CAN BE GOOD

AND ULTIMATELY, LOVE RULES!

Remembering and cherishing this day…and that LOVE RULES!

Obedience Will Follow

Galatians 2:19
"What actually took place is this: I tried keeping rules and working my head off to please God, and it didn't work."

Trying to keep the law perfectly is a useless effort...we can't do it...

I can relate to this verse—for much of my life I tried to earn God's love by being perfectly obedient...I was basically a "law girl," but I gave it up... gave it up to be a "Jesus girl." My identity is in Christ.

I no longer care if I seem to be righteous before you or if I have your good opinion. Nor am I obsessed with impressing God. Christ lives in me! He gave Himself for me!

If I would go back to rule-keeping and peer-pleasing, I would lose everything personal and free that I now have with Jesus. And then Christ would have died unnecessarily.

But He DID die for me! And my love for Him grows deeper each day.

An amazing transformation takes place as my love grows deeper in Christ...obedience seems to follow...through no effort of my own...I am just becoming more and more like Jesus.

Isn't the love of Jesus something wonderful?

Delight

I think we all have a verse we like to claim as "our own." Today, I want to share my life verse with you:

Psalm 37:4
"Delight yourself in the Lord,
And He will give you the desires of your heart." – ESV

This one I call my life verse, because I walk with it every day of my life. Here's why: I am a person who can, at times, wish my life away. Always looking too far down the road and not enjoying the moment…

Always planning…

Always anticipating…

But I hear God speaking to me in this verse, telling me, ***"find your joy, your focus, your heart in Me"****…****"enjoy today," "delight in Me"***—not your life, not your age, not your children's ages…***"look at Me,"*** says the Lord, and ***"I will fulfill it all"***—in His ways, not mine…it is not my map, drawn by me, it is His will, His plan…and His plan is for my good.

Truly, this verse can have sooooo many interpretations, so many different meanings to all the different readers…so I challenge you with my life verse… find yourself in this verse…find yourself in His Word…and guess what you will experience…you know it! **DELIGHT!**

Step Out in Faith

Each day we can look for God's invitation to leave our plans behind to join Him in His great work through us in small steps of obedience.

Here is a thought for you today…

God may not have something HUGE for you to do today…or tomorrow… What if the next "big step" God actually wants you to take is a "small step"?

smile (at everyone, not just those you know)

hope

be a peace-maker

forgive

love

So do that…take small steps today…it may lead to a big leap of faith or it may not…but no matter where you are or what God has called you to do, you can take the first step…

Soundtracks

What is the soundtrack of our lives? Is it "WOW"? Or is it "ehhh"?

Do we truly understand the meaning of the phrase "we carry the very presence of God with us"? Wouldn't that mean that everywhere we go, God is there, BECAUSE we carry His presence with us?

In that case, everywhere I go, He is seen! And wouldn't that make us say, "WOW! How awesome is ***this*** place!"

In our homes—how awesome is ***this*** place!
When we walk into work—how awesome is ***this*** place!
In the grocery store—how awesome is ***this*** place!
At our child's event—how awesome is ***this*** place!
Even picking up my latte/coffee—how awesome is ***this*** place!

Know it and believe it, sweet sisters…you carry the presence of God with you…**WOW…WOW…WOW!**

My Happy Place

Psalm 34:7
"God's angel sets up a circle of protection around us while we pray."

I have this pictured in my mind…do you? God's angel, just for me… covering me with those massive wings…protecting me from everything NOT of God!

every thought…

every word…

every deed…

every evil that desires to devour…

There have been a couple of places that I have named my "happy place," but ***this place***…awwwwww, yes, ***this place IS*** truly my happy place!

Let's take this picture with us in our next moment of prayer. God's angel has circled us with God's protection…what a safe place…such a ***happy place***.

…walk in that moment with thanksgiving and praise…

You Are Precious

Relationships that break can really be hard on a woman.

When this brokenness happens (I think many of us are the same in this), it seems the people closest to us get the worst of us. So on top of the hurt from the broken relationship, we can now layer shame, regret, and a very strange feeling that we may have lost a piece, if not all, of our self. We are convinced that we are not the "special" person we thought we once were. We used to be happy, we used to be an encourager, we used to be strong.

If you find yourself somewhere in here, **stop!** Take a deep breath! And know that you are precious because the Master and Creator of the universe SAYS SO! Reclaim yourself!

Remember that you are not responsible for how others act and react. You ***are*** in control of your own actions and reactions.

Pray diligently in this and hang on to the One who declares you precious! He knows! Your honest cry for His help will not go unheard!

You are precious, sisters!

Writing on the Wall

Romans 5:5

"And hope will not disappoint us, because God's love has been poured out in our hearts through the Holy Spirit who was given to us." – NASB

I'm here to tell you today that the "writing on the wall" DOES happen in our lives.

I woke up this morning with a situation that was concerning on my heart. I have spent a lot of time in my life living in a gap between fear and hope…the enemy is busy in that gap, I'm just sayin'! I prepared for my day with thoughts, many thoughts filling my head regarding the situation. I went to my "special spot" to hear from God—just like every other day…today's reading?…yep, ***Romans 5:5***…I felt a warming in my spirit…I looked up and right at eye level straight in front of me was a plaque…simple writing on it…**HOPE**…only that—**HOPE**. I have three plaques on different places on the walls in this room, each having one word on them…***hope, joy, and faith***…but today **HOPE** stared me in the face…the writing on the wall…"this hope will not disappoint us."

Listen for Him, ladies! He is speaking into your heart today. Watch for it! Expect Him to write on the wall!

High Five

Recently we celebrated "national high-five day." I really am not sure who gets to establish these days, but anyway, we had some fun giving each other a few high fives…and I got some in to God as well! Yes, ladies, totally appropriate to high five God!

On the same day, while reading, I came across a phrase: "raise up a standard of righteousness in this land"…I love this phrase, and it kind of reminded me of the whole "high-five" thing going on. But back to the phrase: ***"raise up a standard of righteousness in this land."***

How can we apply this?

Maybe we encourage each other instead of criticizing.
Maybe we give our boss our hardest day of work yet.
Let's tell the truth instead of that little white lie.
Maybe we go out of our way to make someone else's day better.
Maybe we smile instead of frown.
Or pick up that piece of trash instead of letting someone else do it.

Now this is truly a list that never ends!
Let's be the one, sisters! Let's make a difference!

Let today be a day we ***"raise up a standard of righteousness in this land."***

Letting Go

Hebrews 10:23
"Without wavering, let us hold tight to the hope we say we have, for God can be trusted to keep His promise." – NLT

When I am discouraged or frustrated, it usually isn't because my life is awful. Most often it's because I feel God isn't doing what I think He should. He hasn't really followed "my designed plan" for my life or the lives of my family and friends.

"...God can be trusted to keep His promise."

I'm growing in my understanding that the amount I enjoy God as well as enjoy my life directly relates to how much I trust God in my life.

"...God can be trusted..."

It really is all about ***letting go*** and trusting God...

One More Thing

2 Thessalonians 3:1–2
"One more thing, friends; Pray for us. Pray that the Master's Word will simply take off and race through the country to a groundswell of response, just as it did among you. And pray that we'll be rescued from these scoundrels who are trying to do us in."

The day I read this verse was a "dark day" in the country I live in. Its words are so very real…***"these scoundrels who are trying to do us in"***…

Our response is so needed, sisters! ***"Pray…pray that the Master's Word will simply take off and race through the country to a groundswell of response…and that we'll be rescued…"***

"One more thing," sisters: **"pray"!**

Be You

Since the beginning of time there has never been another with the mind, heart, eyes, ears, hands, hair, and mouth that you have. No one that ***has*** lived, ***is*** living, or ***will*** live can walk and talk, move and think exactly like you.

Not one other person can duplicate your handwriting, produce your child, duplicate your brush strokes.

You are unique, one of a kind. You are rare and there is great value in that!

The same is true in reverse—all attempts for you to imitate others will fail as well.

So celebrate YOU today, sisters!

You are here for a purpose. A unique purpose that only you can fulfill! And no one, **NO ONE** can do it but you!

BE YOU!

Listen, Listen

Isaiah 30:21

"Whether you turn to the right or to the left, your ears will hear a voice behind you, saying, 'This is the way; walk in it.'" – NIV

This is such a great verse! And I am wondering how many of us have actually invited the Holy Spirit into each step we take? There is so much benefit to be enjoyed when we do.

A gal asked me if I hear the Spirit speaking to me. Yes, yes, I do. But that doesn't mean I always listen, pay attention, or heed what I hear. (I'm a work in progress!)

Several people have said to me lately, "I wish I could hear God speaking to me." This is a good start!

Today, ladies, I want to challenge you to invite the Spirit to speak to you. At the same time, ask God to open your ears and your heart to be tuned in to the Spirit.

…listen with your head…listen with your heart…and just maybe your ears too…

The Abraham Adventure

There may be a season in your life when God calls you to an adventure such as Abraham experienced. A time when you feel God asking you to make a big move! This could be a physical, emotional, or even spiritual move. Part of it feels very exciting (that is, if you are prone to embrace a good adventure), but part of it feels like you are leaving your best behind, and that can bring a bit of anxiousness.

I feel your heart, sister! The ***unknown*** doesn't feel particularly safe, yet the opportunity to experience something new and different can be very alluring. I know if you are walking this path, you know exactly what I am saying.

It may mean that you are physically leaving family and friends, it may mean that your relationships and once close friends will change, and even you yourself are now moving into ***new*** close relationships. It may mean that you are being challenged by a personality trait that needs adjusting, or you are being called to leave an addiction that in a strange way has felt like "home" to you. Or, it may even mean that God has awakened your heart to a whole new experience of who He is and is asking you to join Him on that spiritual adventure.

There are really so many possibilities, and these are only a few. I can only say, don't grieve where you have been. Embrace where you have been because it has brought you to where you are. Where you are is taking you to new close relationships, to a better you, to a deeper faith in Him.

Genesis 17:7

"I'm establishing my covenant between me and you, a covenant that includes your descendants, a covenant that goes on and on and on, a covenant that commits me to be your God and the God of your descendants."

Ladies, Abraham's journey was worth the taking. Don't be afraid. Your God is with you…and your children…and your children's children…

Altars

I have the luxury of a few very quiet moments…all is calm, all is well… and I am sitting with some alone time…

I wonder how many of you keep notes on your thoughts…some call this journaling…I would just classify myself as a "thought keeper." I'm not as consistent as I picture a person that consistently journals, but I like to capture my "ah-ha" moments and write them down.

Every now and then I like to review my thoughts…it very much reminds me of the people in the Bible who established ***altars*** to remember God in one way or another. Exactly one year ago I made special notes about this verse:

1 Samuel 14:6
"Nothing can hinder the Lord from saving, not by many or by few."

I remember the exact situation and remember very well what happened not long after…It's a good reminder to me of the faithfulness of God…a good reminder…an ***altar***…

I thanked Him today for His faithfulness as I saw it one year ago…and it gives me hope for His presence in what I am facing today…In my opinion, this is one time when looking back can encourage my spirit.

I encourage you, ladies, to keep track of your ***altars*** in whatever way works for you, and then be reminded of how you saw God in that time in your life. Use these altars to draw encouragement for today…for tomorrow…

Your heart will be blessed by how many ***altars*** you have been able to build on your journey…your spirit will be refreshed by His faithfulness along the way.

Shine Bright

Psalm 38:9
"Lord, my longings are sitting in plain sight, my groans an old story to you. My heart's about to break: I'm a burned-out case."

Without all of the details, ladies, there is a gal who needs our prayers. I am calling on all of you who read this to say a sweet prayer for our desperate friend.

Sometimes, life is just hard. We have all had times when our spirits have been lifted by the prayers of others. Well, now we have the opportunity to lift the spirits of another sister…it is the whole idea of "blessed to be a blessing" put into action.

So as you quickly pass by this, ask God to break through the darkness that our sister feels has surrounded her life! Pray that her life will again shine bright in knowing the resurrection power of our Lord, Jesus Christ! Praise God for this gal, and the power of praise will invite God into the middle of her life to act for His Kingdom and her good.

To my friend, my sister in Christ, feel His love today. Let joy capture your heart knowing who you are in Christ. May His presence be your center today!

Bless you, sister, on your journey…

One More Step

There are times in my life when I think I have made a major breakthrough in my faith walk, and it feels so significant that I think I need to share this really great new thing with others. It's as though I have discovered a hidden scroll with answers that I have been searching for. The truth being, there really is nothing new about it. It has been here since creation.

Thus, my experience last evening. I was privileged to meet with a special group for reflection. A couple of breakthroughs for me, really. The first one is that prayer is conversation with God (nothing new there). BUT! That means if I believe God's presence is in me, any conversation I have with anyone is prayer, since God is there. Read that again, please—kinda changes some of my conversations with the people I rub shoulders with in my day.

Second, when I praise God for each and every situation, I have invited Him into the middle of the situation. This is freedom for me! Sometimes in my conversations with God, I find myself desperate, pleading, and almost instructing Him on what needs to be done in this or that situation. BUT! When I praise God for that tough relationship, for a bad habit, for a weak tendency, etc., I invite Him in the middle to do what only He can do. And because He is in the middle of the situation, I have just prayed a blessing into it. Oh, I hope this makes sense to you, because it is a life-changer for me! My heart smiles. I feel humble and so very thankful for who our God is!

It's just one more step on my rugged, dusty, and getting to be well-worn path.

Oh, sisters, I praise God you are walking with me…

The Match Game

This one might sting a bit, ladies, but 1 John 2:4 is in my face today… ***"Be sure your life matches your words"***…see what I mean?

We've heard this other ways, like "walk the talk," and I know you know more expressions too…we're gals, we love a good conversation, right?

We love our opinion…we love our side of a story…we give advice… we LOVE to give advice…so much sweeter to give advice than to receive it, right?

Well, as we so freely dish it out, let's check ourselves…so easy for us to say:

"you need to get over it"
"you need to forgive them"
"you need to quit spending"
"you need to be optimistic"
"you need to be honest"
(I need a latte—this really hurts.)

Maybe receiving advice is tough because we don't see the person giving the advice living it themselves. OUCH!

….does this mean fewer words? Hmmmmmm…possibly…some situations maybe…but let's take the advice this man, John, was inspired to write…

"Be sure your life matches your words."

Does Grace Have Limits?

I have to say that a good latte MUST have been part of creation...so much good conversation takes place with one in front of me...

Today, a dear friend and a good question..."Is there a limit to God's grace?"

"Surely there are some limits."

"Where does God draw the line?"

"Is there EVER a case where grace just has to go too far, when God shakes His head and turns His back?"

This from the gentle heart of a concerned mama...my answer: I in no way can or ever will declare to know the mind, the intentions of God, Himself... BUT, this I know...grace found me...and I hold on to His Word...especially 2 Peter 2:9—"The Lord does not delay His promise, as some understand delay, but is patient with you, not wanting any to perish but all to come to repentance"...when His Word says "all," I believe He means "ALL." There is no limit to the long arms of the Lord...He will go as far or as deep as needed to bring a precious lamb back home...

Peace, sweet friend...God sees your precious child...

God's Gift

This morning I am just going to use His Words (always a good decision, right?)

Ephesians 2:7–10
"Now God has us where He wants us, with all the time in this world and the next to shower grace and kindness upon us in Christ Jesus. Saving is all His idea, and all His work. All we do is trust Him enough to let Him do it. It's God's gift from start to finish! We don't play the major role. If we did, we'd probably go around bragging that we'd done the whole thing! No, we neither make nor save ourselves. God does both the making and the saving. He creates each of us by Christ Jesus to join Him in the work He does, the good work He has gotten ready for us to do, work we had better be doing."

It says it right there…"it's a gift"—"God's gift," and He has made sure we lack nothing for the season we are in right now…

Are You Hungry?

For a brief period of time some friends and I are scooting our chairs a little closer to the book of Hebrews. A great question was brought up: "How hungry for God are you in this season of your life?" On a scale of one to ten, where would you place yourself? And what would the people who are closest to us in this season say we are craving? Physical peace? Financial security? Emotional strength? Resolution in a difficult relationship? Peace for our children? More of Jesus? What are we hungry for? And what has made us hungry for God in the past? (You may need that cup of coffee and that quiet space here.)

Let's not be too quick to leave this chair…what is getting our attention right now? What am I craving more than Him?

Psalm 63:5

"You satisfy me as with rich food; my mouth will praise You with joyful lips."

He satisfies my hunger…write it down, say it over and over…He satisfies me…

Hush That Murmur

Philippians 4:11
"I have learned in whatever state I am, therewith to be content." – KJV

You just know that when a verse hits you twice in a very short period of time, you better pay particular attention...welcome Philippians 4:11. Be content...here's the thing...none of us need to be taught how to complain. It seems that it comes quite naturally...kinda like weeds in a garden...we may be hoping for the beautiful flower garden, but we know it will take some work to keep out the weeds if we want to enjoy the beauty that the flowers were meant to bring...

Contentment is a beautiful flower in our life and only our "new nature" can produce it. Even then we have to be very purposeful in maintaining it... no doubt there will be seasons when we think we don't have any weeds in our garden...yep, we are content...and then, oops! We spot one—maybe just a little weed, but funny how soon it multiplies...not long after, we hear ourselves complaining...

Let's start today...hush the murmurs...a day of encouragement...a day of compliments...counting the blessings...a day of contentment...today...

Do the Better Thing

2 Corinthians 9:6
"He who sows sparingly and grudgingly will also reap sparingly and grudgingly, and he who sows generously will also reap generously and with blessings."

A two-dollar tip on a $6 breakfast?…I have two $1 bills…and here I sit, tormented…$1 does not seem enough…$2 seems a bit over the top…$1.50 feels just right…do I need to get change? How much time have I wasted considering my options? I don't really think the $0.50 would make that much difference to this sweet young waitress, but, then again, the message may mean everything to her! It says "thank you." It says what she does is important!

The Word says the generous person will always be blessed. An amazing opportunity for us! Bringing joy with mere pocket change! Sometimes the little things have huge results! An unexpected compliment, holding a door open, a smile—all cost us very little, but oh, the blessings we receive…

Today, do the better thing…

What Time Is It?

Today I am sitting under Acts 1…sit with me a bit, would ya? Paul is talking of the last days of Christ—the final scene before Jesus ascended to Heaven. The disciples ask Jesus, "Master, are you going to restore the kingdom to Israel now? Is this the time?" Jesus tells them, "You don't get to know the time. Timing is the Father's business. What you will get is the Holy Spirit."

I don't mean to take anything out of context…but the words, His Words, just jumped off the page…"Is this the time?" "You don't get to know the time. Timing is the Father's business." How many times do we wrestle with God's timing? We ask…we wait…and wait…and we become anxious, restless…even doubtful…then we think He most certainly must not have heard us, so we ask again…and wait…we can spend a lot of time and energy right here…when what Jesus says is, "What you will get is the Holy Spirit." To help us get up…to move forward…to have hope…to have joy…and peace…even courage…maybe the answer is to stop worrying about the time and focus on the Spirit…His power…His strength…moving us forward…making us stronger…

As we step out today, let's lay down "time" and pick up "power"…His mighty power…

Coach's Corner

If you are in need of a good pep talk today, check out Isaiah 61—in any version really. I have had many coaches in my life with many pep talks, but Isaiah's is one of the best. Just some highlights: "His Spirit is on me"—better than any Powerade I know of…and then the game plan—tell the good news, share the freedom, celebrate God's grace, care for the needy, bring messages of joy, have a heart of praise, rebuild the ruins…hey! All things I can do in the power the Spirit gives me! And the victory? The prize? We ALL love a prize! We will be "honored as ministers of our God"! We will "feast on the bounty of nations"! Our "inheritance in the land will be doubled" and our "joy will go on forever"!

I want to be on that team!
Feel the adrenaline? Put me in, coach!

Let's Talk

Psalm 27:8
"My heart has heard you say, 'Come talk with me.' And my heart responds, 'Lord, I am coming.'"

Such a sweet verse…a tender invitation to have that needed convo with our Father…said in such a loving way…

Let's talk. Life is overwhelming?

Let's talk. Is there sickness?

Let's talk. Questions?

Let's talk. Great, great joy?

Let's talk. Frustrated?

Betrayed? Surprised? Excited? Amazed?

Just have some time?

Let's talk. Can you see it? His open arms? His kind eyes and sweet smile? Picture Him in just this moment…in just this way…

Lord, I am coming…Lord, we are coming…

Consider Jesus

A line from one of my favorite movies, starring Tom Hanks and Meg Ryan, is (Tom Hanks speaking): "The answer to every question is...," and he completes that with a reference from the movie *The Godfather*. The writer in Hebrews 3:1 is saying the answer to every question is "Consider Jesus!" This simple command to turn our eyes to Jesus is the answer to every situation...to every broken or hurtful relationship... to every injustice we feel and see...whenever we feel exhausted, anxious, hopeless...even angry...the answer to every question is Jesus...say it louder—JESUS!

JESUS spoken into any situation is the right answer! The name above ALL names...JESUS!

Jesus!

And say it with each step today!

He Is Our God

Jeremiah 31:33
"I will be their God."

This is a moment of celebration and a challenge all in one very short sentence! Celebrate! He IS my God! Yay! Insert cartwheels…but…and there it is…but, is that enough? He is my God…do I desire anything or anyone else? I say I don't…if I pour that into my cup, is it full? Does it overflow? What is it that keeps me looking for more? Something on this earth promises me more than the joy of Heaven? The attractions and the distractions of this earth just can't compare with "He is my God"! I read once that this alone should make my heart beat wildly and my eyes sparkle…does it?

Let's just breathe in those words—His words—today…"He is my God"…breathe in deeply…now exhale…exhale anything that dares to attract or distract us…divine breathing…that's what our plan is today. He is my God…in and out…He is my God…

Mountaintop Experience

Philippians 4:12
"I know how to abound."

Do you find yourself longing for mountaintop experiences? I wonder… do we know how to abound? Do we know how to live on that mountaintop? The apostle says it is a divine lesson to know how to be full and to be hungry. I'm thinking it may be harder for us to be full than to be hungry…there is no doubt we know when we need Him, right? But what are we like when He has answered our prayer? Shown His mercy? Met our need?…when I am full?…do I celebrate for a bit and then forget?…we just have such a tendency toward pride and forgetfulness toward God…I tell myself I so want to be full…and oh, I don't want to be hungry…

I'm going to need the power of the Spirit for this, but Lord, teach me how to be full…how to abound.

Are you full? Are you hungry? Lord, teach us…

He Is My Deliverer

Genesis 50:20
"You intended to harm me, but God intended it all for good. He brought me to this position so I could save the lives of many people." – ESV

Let's grab a cup of coffee and just sit under this one for a bit...I wear a bracelet made by a young girl in a third-world country...it is made of bullets...bullets that chase her down...she gathers these stray bullets and makes bracelets to sell to provide for herself and her small family in the name of Jesus...what the devil meant for harm, God has made good...

Such a good reminder to me that when the devil is chasing and attacking me and my loved ones...what the devil means for harm, God has made for good...take a sip of that coffee and let its warmth and HIS soothe the chill you feel...

Today, as you walk it out...

Trust Him...He IS our Deliverer...

Shadows to the Substance

Colossians 2:2
"I want you woven into a tapestry of love, in touch with everything there is to know of God. All the richest treasures of wisdom and knowledge are embedded in that mystery and nowhere else."

Picture us being "woven" in that tapestry…do our colors stand out? Hmmmmmm…

Colossians 2:7
"You're deeply rooted in Him. You're well constructed upon Him. You know your way around faith. Now do what you've been taught. School's out; quit studying the subject and start living it! And let your living spill over in thanksgiving."

These words are a little tougher for me because I don't feel I am near ready to quit learning…in ways I still crave the "milk"…but I love the challenge laid out—school's out! Live it! Flip the switch! Just DO it!

Colossians 2:10–12
"You don't need a telescope, a microscope, or a horoscope to realize the fullness of Christ, and the emptiness of the universe without Him. When you come to Him, that fullness comes together for you, too. His power extends over everything. Entering into this fullness is not something you figure out or achieve. It's not a matter of being circumcised or keeping a long list of laws. No, you're already in—insiders—not through some secretive initiation rite but rather through what Christ has already gone through for you, destroying the power of sin. If it's an initiation ritual you're after, you've already been through it by submitting to baptism."

Shadows to the Substance, continued

We don't need to stress out about finding Him…feeling desperate in a search for Him…just open our hearts…receive Him…

I was going to leave this last part out, but…

Colossians 2:16–23
"So don't put up with anyone pressuring you in details of diet, worship services, holy days…Do you think things that are here today and gone tomorrow are worth that kind of attention? Such things sound impressive if said in a deep enough voice. They even give the illusion of being pious and humble and ascetic. But they're just another way of showing off, making yourselves look important."

A good reminder for me to NOT lay this kind of pressure on people I share life with. Let God, by the power of the Spirit, and the great love of Jesus, sow the work on the inside…what the world sees on the outside of our lives is a reflection of the inside of our hearts…pray for the change on the inside, for God to be at work there…and maybe we will see the change, the outward reflection…the Word says, we will see the fruit…but let's be in prayer for the heart.

Good reading today! And as we know, we will never come away from His Word empty! Praise you, Lord!

Celebrate our great God!

Pray for Open Doors

Colossians 4:5–6

"Use your heads as you live and work among outsiders. Don't miss a trick. Make the most of every opportunity. Be gracious in your speech. The goal is to bring out the best in others in a conversation, not put them down, not cut them out."

Another verse jumped into my head this morning: "*draw them in with cords of kindness*."

We are to be the most loving of all people…not judgmental…not finger pointing…not harsh…and yet, always ready for each opportunity to speak of how the love of Jesus, the mercy and grace of our Father, and the strength of the Spirit has changed and keeps changing us. We are all works in progress… no one should ever feel excluded based on our attitude, actions, or words—all should feel invited to the feast with the King!

Do you find yourself being judgmental?

Convictions of Steel

The words jumped off the page at me today.

1 Thessalonians
Verse 1 – The last three words are "God's robust peace." One of the earlier books talked of "robust trust"—really starting to like that word!
Verse 4 – "It is clear to us, friends, that God not only loves you very much but also has put his hand on you for something special."
Verse 5 – "When the Message we preached came to you, it wasn't just words. Something happened in you. The Holy Spirit put steel in your convictions."

I love this very strong picture…sometimes my faith seems more like soft butter…I'm gonna concentrate on "steel," not "butter"!

…walking in a full covering of ***steel*** today…

Do you walk in butter or steel?

Lifting Each Other Up

1 Thessalonians 3

What a letter of encouragement for how we lift each other up…sometimes it is actions and words to encourage…but sometimes it is in us watching faith-filled individuals walk through difficult times…it can really encourage us as well.

Verse 11–13
"May God our Father Himself and our Master Jesus clear the road to you! And may the Master pour on the love so it fills your lives and splashes over on everyone around you, just as it does from us to you. May you be infused with strength and purity, filled with confidence in the presence of God our Father when our Master Jesus arrives with all His followers."

These are my words of encouragement as well as my prayer for each of you!

Blessings!

Lazy?

2 Thessalonians 3

Title in the Message: "Those Who Are Lazy"

I am taking this one to heart and applying it in all areas of my life:

Don't be lazy…
In my devotions
Attending to my family
In church activities
In my community involvement
In His Kingdom work
In my friendships
Tending to my health and wellness
…and of course at my place of employment…

God has created me to be "purposeful"…He favors my efforts in His name…yes, He gives me times at rest as well…but rest is different than being lazy. It feels like one is needed and the other is a choice. An excuse…

I looked at this chapter and thought, "Oh, this must just be a quick closer." WOW! A lot of power in just a few words, right! Just like God…

In the list above is there an area that you tend to be lazy?

Not My Will, but Thine

Luke 22:42

We are challenged today to write down the things that make us angry for why God has allowed them to happen…write down the things that we have questions about that we just can't understand…write them all down.

It's not wrong to talk to God about these things…let's talk to Him about them all…God, why this?…Why not this? And then when we are done, let's lay them down with Jesus' own words…

Father, I would like another way, BUT!

"Not my will, but thine, be done."

And know that He has heard and His will is perfect for you…
Step out in His perfect will for you today!

In His Grip

2 Thessalonians 2

Well, verses 1–12 were not for the faint of heart…all those situations that must take place are VERY dark!

But verses 13–17 are the ***"glorious sun"*** or rather SON on a very dark day!

"Meanwhile, we've got our hands full continually thanking God for you, our good friends—so loved by God! God picked you out as his from the very start. Think of it: included in God's original plan of salvation by the bond of faith in the living truth. This is the life of the Spirit he invited you to through the Message we delivered, in which you get in on the glory of our Master, Jesus Christ. So friends, take a firm stand, feet on the ground and head high. Keep a tight grip on what you were taught, whether in personal conversation or by our letter. May Jesus himself and God our Father, who reached out in love and surprised you with gifts of unending help and confidence, put a fresh heart in you, invigorate your work, enliven your speech."

…in His tight grip!
Walking with the Lord is a daily walk. We are kept in His tight grip.

Walking in His Energy

A couple of things jumped off the page today for me:

2 Thessalonians 1:6–7
"When the Master Jesus appears out of heaven in a blaze of fire with his strong angels, he'll even up the score by settling accounts with those who gave you such a bad time. His coming will be the break we've been waiting for!"

Title of this section is "Justice Is on the Way"—I think we all celebrate justice…but a gentle reminder to me as well.

2 Thessalonians 1:11–12
"Because we know that this extraordinary day is just ahead, we pray for you all the time—pray that our God will make you fit for what he's called you to be, pray that he'll fill your good ideas and acts of faith with his own energy so that it all amounts to something. If your life honors the name of Jesus, he will honor you."

…walking today in His energy…
How do you keep walking in His energy?

My Heart Is Light and Full

Verse 1 – "Keep doing what we told you to do to please God, not in a dogged religious pod, but in a living, 'spirited dance.'"
Verse 4 – "Learn to appreciate and give dignity to your body, not abusing it..."
Verse 6 – "Don't run roughshod over the concerns of your brothers and sisters. Their concerns are God's concerns and He will take care of them...God hasn't invited us into a disorderly, unkempt life but into something holy and beautiful—as beautiful on the inside as the outside."

...and then, what a finale!

Verse 15–18 – "'We have the Master's word on it. He IS coming!' And the Message says, 'We will be walking on air'"!

How amazing! How exciting!

...we are dancing and will be walking on air...my heart feels light and FULL!

How do you remain walking on air?

The Glory

I find myself praising our Father today…not because life is easy…but because He rolled the stone away…because I have life because He lives… because He lives, I can face…whatever…I know He holds my future in His hands…

1 Peter 4:12–13
"Friends, when life gets really difficult, don't jump to the conclusion that God isn't on the job. Instead, be glad that you are in the very thick of what Christ experienced. This is a spiritual refining process, with glory just around the corner."

…glory just around the corner…

Walking in faith, hope, and love…because He did…
Let others know that walking in faith is a glorious journey.

When You Open Your Mouth

James 3:1

"We get it wrong nearly every time we open our mouths."

True? What a challenge for us…well, for me, anyways. Many times I find I open my mouth with unnecessary words…silly words…maybe not mean words, but just space fillers and really NOT needed…

James 3:17

"Real wisdom, God's wisdom, begins with a holy life and is characterized by getting along with others. It is gentle and reasonable, overflowing with mercy and blessings, not hot one day and cold the next."

I go back to my life motto here: "If you know it and it doesn't change your life then you don't really know it." Our wisdom is shown by our actions…a good challenge to begin this morning…

WISDOM = ACTIONS

Blessings, sisters!

Life From Within

From the Message, the title of James 5 is "Destroying Your Life From Within." This caught my attention right away!

How very sad…when God has placed us in a beautiful place with sustenance abounding, along with the joy of working for the Almighty One, that we would still destroy ourselves with our heart and mind…oh Holy Spirit, keep our heart and mind centered and focused on Him who is able to do all things in a greater way than we can imagine or dream!

Then verses 19–20 also: *"My dear friends, if you know people who have wandered off from God's truth, don't write them off. Go after them! Get them back and you will have rescued precious lives from destruction and prevented an epidemic of wandering away from God."*

I know this is something you have all heard from me many times, but I feel we, as the church family, really stink at this. How quick we are to point a finger, kick someone out of the family…and we call this Biblical discipline… that is NOT what I read here…we are to go after them, pursue them, draw them back…not punish, criticize, or judge. I just have such a heart for those who have been drawn away from the community of faith by hurt, anger, or the world…let's be how they find their way back to Jesus!

…how can I be a road map back home?

How do you make people feel welcomed?

Encouragers

1 Thessalonians 5:4
"We are Daughters of Day. We live under wide open skies and know where we stand. So let's not sleepwalk through life…but keep our eyes open."
Verse 12 – "Honor your leaders who work so hard for you…overwhelm them with appreciation and love."

Let's silence the criticism and be overwhelming encouragers!

Look for ways to cooperate…and possibly challenge or invite a "free-loader" to join us in a project.

Verse 13 – "Get along among yourselves, each of you doing your part. Look for the best in each other, and always do your best to bring it out."

Don't suppress the Spirit; rather, cooperate with the Spirit the next time He asks you to participate in a Christian meeting.

My notes on these verses say, "a word of encouragement offered at the right moment can be the difference between finishing well and collapsing along the way…our journey continues…look around you! Be sensitive to those around you and offer support words or actions."

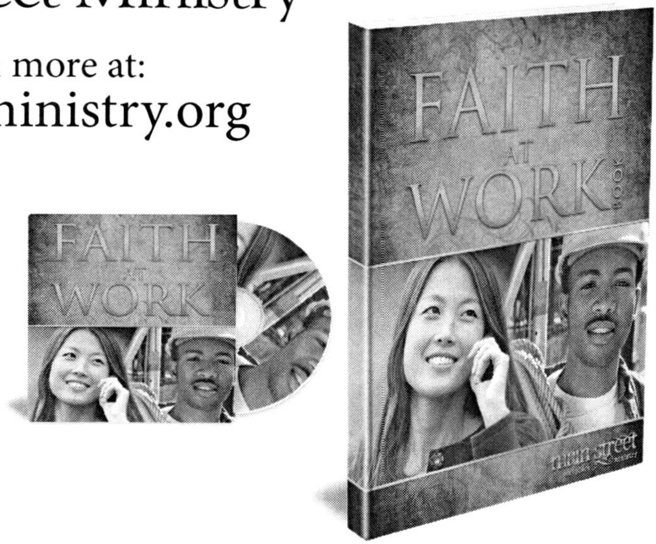

FAITH AT WORK
FAITH AT WORK BOOK

HEARING GOD AT WORK
SABRA DYAS
WISDOM
THE PROVERBS AT WORK
VOLUME I
Sabra Dyas
HEARING GOD AS A TEEN
SABRA DYAS

FAITH AT WORK DEVOTIONAL SERIES
ALTARS
FAITH AT WORK DEVOTIONAL SERIES
TREASURES
Sabra Dyas

CPSIA information can be obtained
at www.ICGtesting.com
Printed in the USA
FSOW02n0007271215
14976FS

9 780996 825009